M000205190

The
Peacocks of Palos Verdes
Mary Jo Hazard, M.A., M.F.T.

Photographs

Bryce Lowe-White

DONEGAL PUBLISHING COMPANY
LOS ANGELES

❀❀❀❀❀❀

Copyright © 2010 by Mary Jo Hazard

All rights reserved. No part of this publication, except for brief excerpts for purpose of review, may be reproduced, stored in a retrieval system, or transmitted in any form or by any means, electronic, mechanical, photocopying, recording, or otherwise without the prior written permission of the publisher.

Donegal Publishing Company, LLC
1850 Industrial Street, #307
Los Angeles, CA 90021
Email: editor@donegalpublishing.com
www.donegalpublishing.com
TEL (310) 598-6340
FAX (310) 349-3441

All Donegal books are available via your favorite bookstore, amazon.com, or from our 24 hour order website: www.donegalbooks.com

Library of Congress Control Number: 2010922063
Publisher's Cataloging—in—Publication Data
The Peacocks of Palos Verdes/Mary Jo Hazard, M.A., M.F.T.
   1st ed.—Los Angeles, California: Donegal Publishing Company, LLC, 2010
      p. ; cm.
      ISBN 13 : 978-0-9788128-3-6
      ISBN 10 : 0-9788128-3-2
      1. California —Palos Verdes—Juvenile Non-Fiction. 2. Palos Verdes—History—Juvenile Non-Fiction.3. Peacocks—Juvenile Non-Fiction. 4. Photography—Non-Fiction. I. Hazard, Mary Jo. II. Title.

This book was written, designed, printed and bound in the United States of America.
To order additional copies, please visit: www.PeacocksOfPalosVerdes.com

PPI/Logan, Iowa, USA   01/10, 309135

Foreword

The peacocks of Palos Verdes have graced our seaside community for nearly 100 years. Their origins can be traced to the peninsula's original developer, Frank Vanderlip, who was presented with the original six pairs of peafowl to "liven up" his otherwise self-described "too quiet" new home in Portuguese Bend in 1916. And liven things up they did! As the peafowl families grew, the males began to spread out in search of new territory, which, until the 1950s, remained mostly undeveloped rural hillsides, canyons and chaparral, inhabited only by the most adventurous families who left the city for the country life.

The wild peafowl living on the Peninsula today, descendents of those original six pairs, have graciously continued to share their habitat with the increasing number of humans who have since flocked to our beautiful area. We are fortunate to have inherited both the pleasure and the responsibility of preserving this unique keep-sake of the early days of Palos Verdes. It is our intention that Frank Vanderlip's legacy of peacocks in Palos Verdes continues enlivening our community for our children, and their children's children to cherish.

Deborah McKinney Mott, President
Friends of the Peacock, Inc.
www.friendsofthepeacock.org

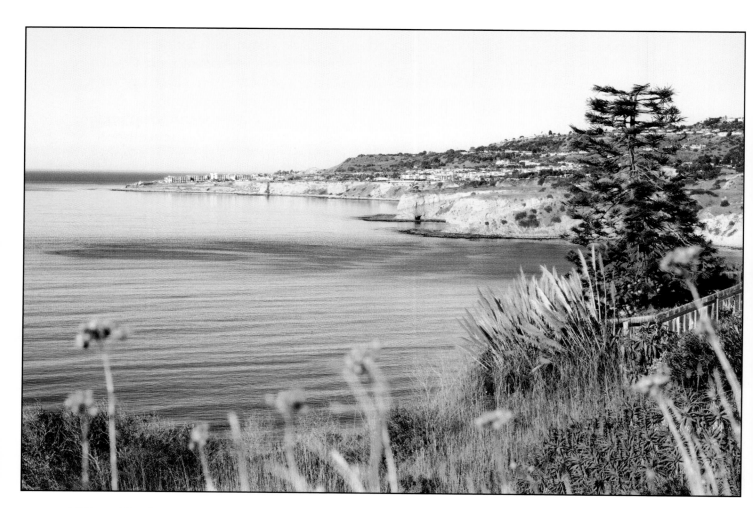

The Palos Verdes Peninsula has many sights to see,
crashing waves, rolling hills and peacocks in the trees.

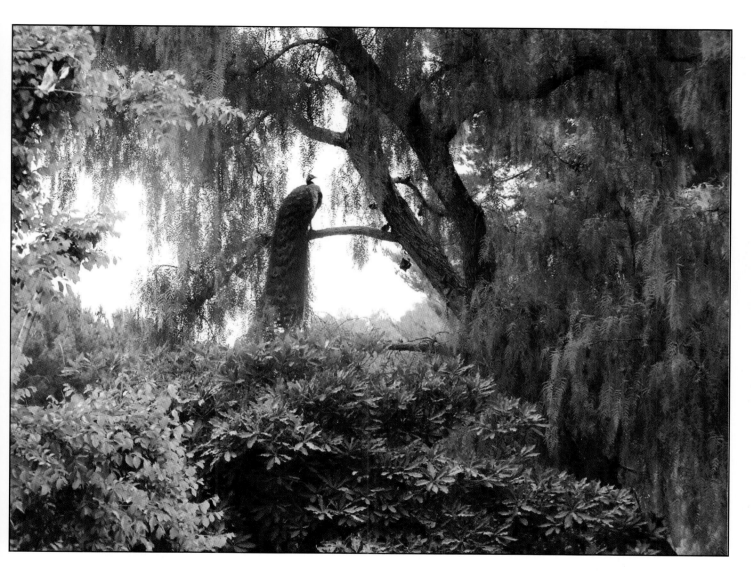

Yes, peacocks in the trees...

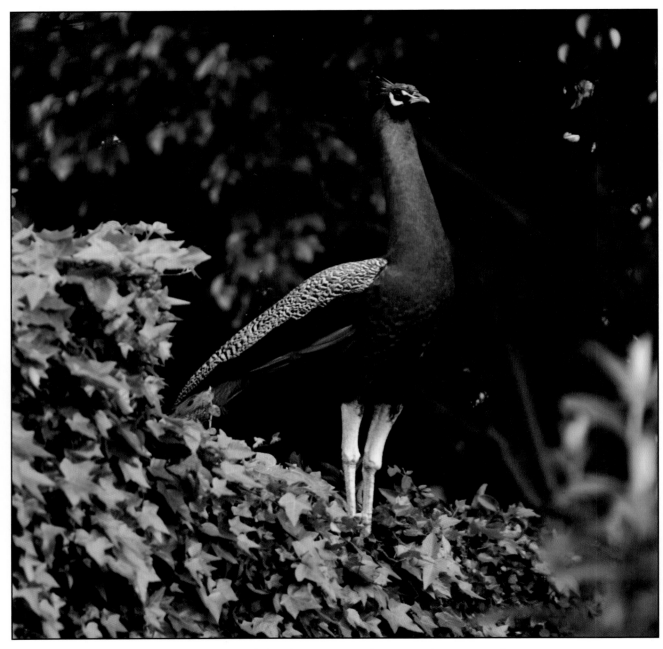

Peacocks are birds, stately and proud.
Their voices are shrill and frightfully loud.

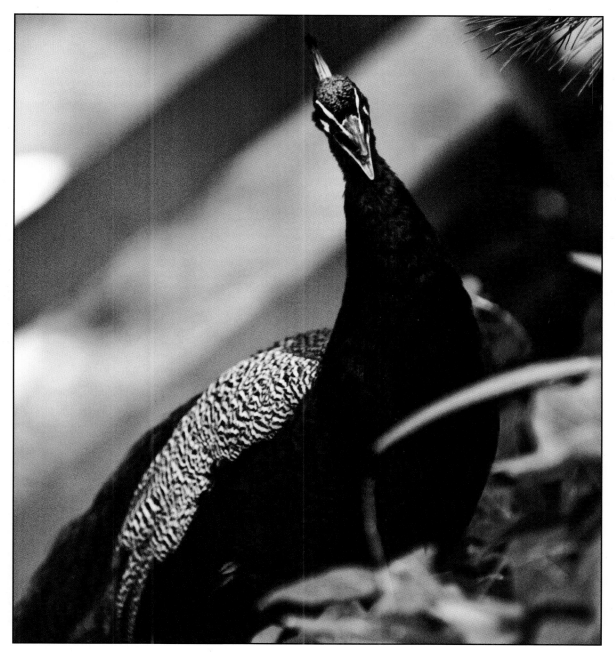

"Look at me! Look at me!" males scream and shout,
then all of a sudden their tails fan out.

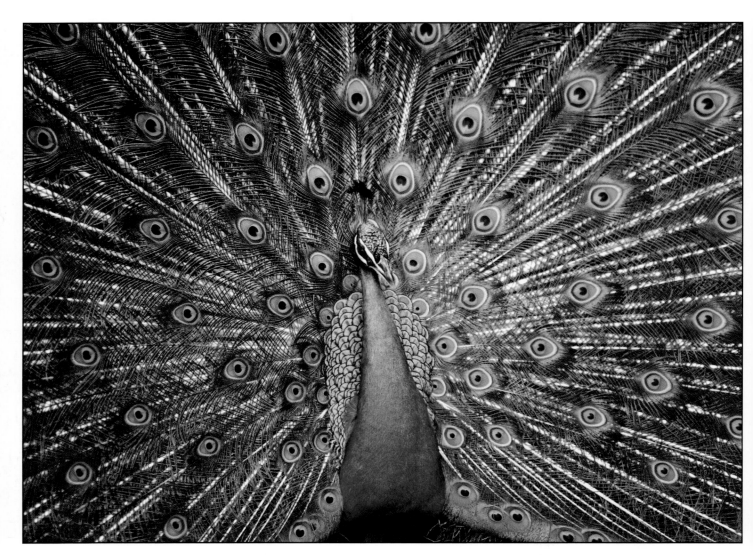

Their fans are gigantic — some reach six feet high.

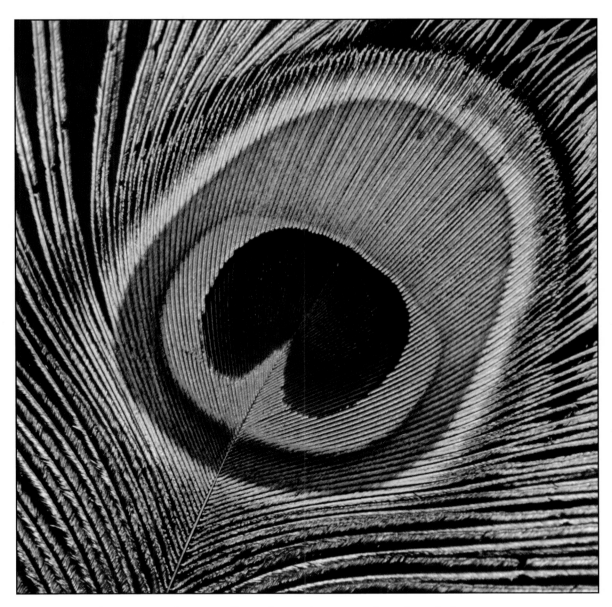

And every long feather is marked with an eye.

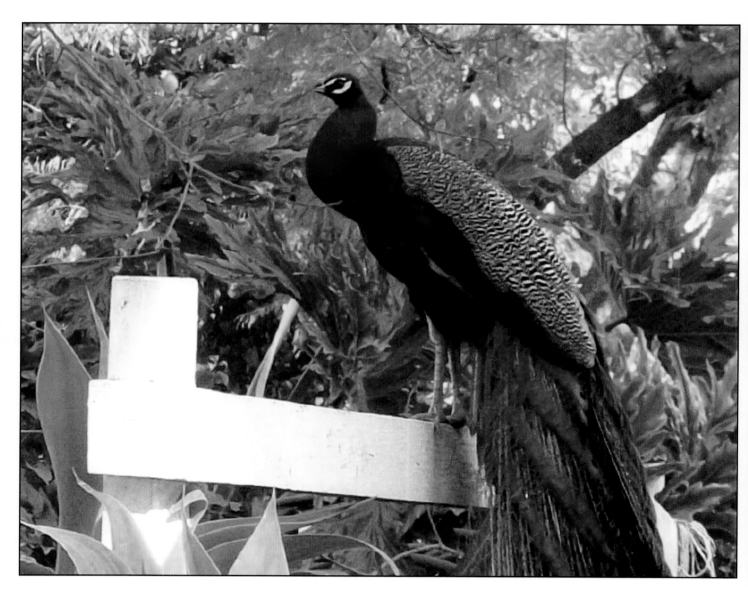

They perch on fences and roost in trees.

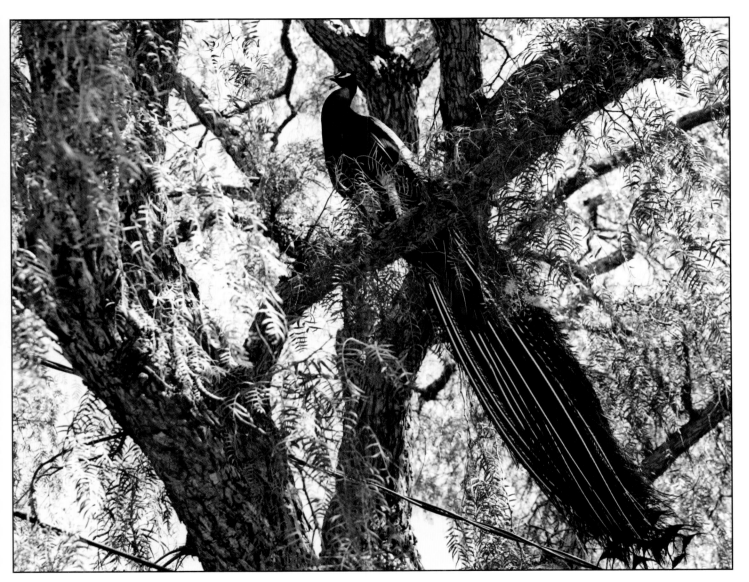

Their trains hang down and swing in the breeze.

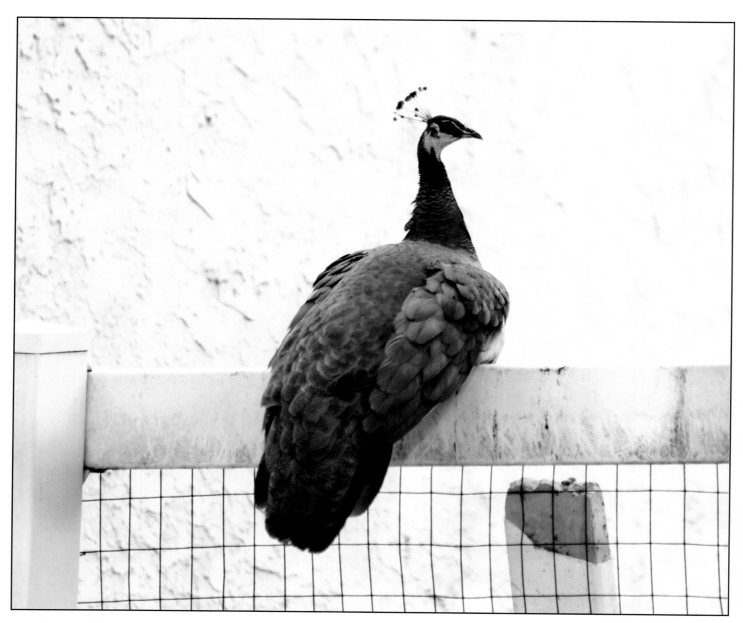

The peahens are drab, light brown, green and gray.
Their tails are so short that their feathers don't sway.

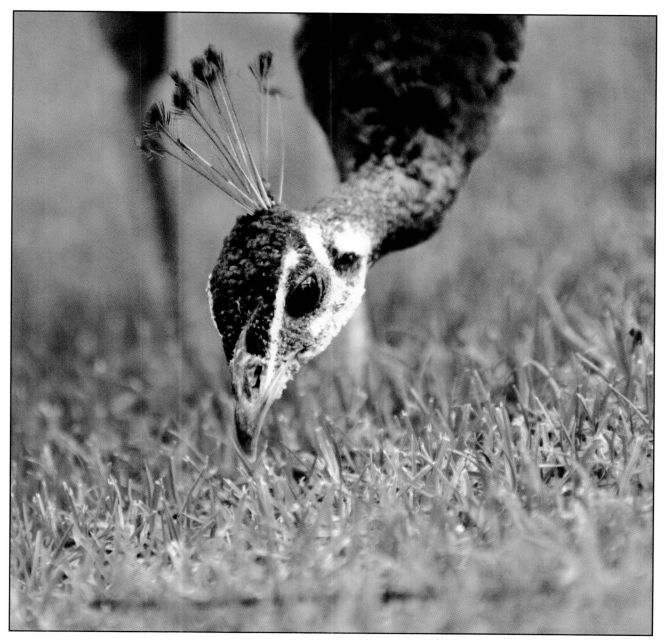

Peacocks eat lizards, crickets, and ants.
They gobble up snakes and love eating plants.

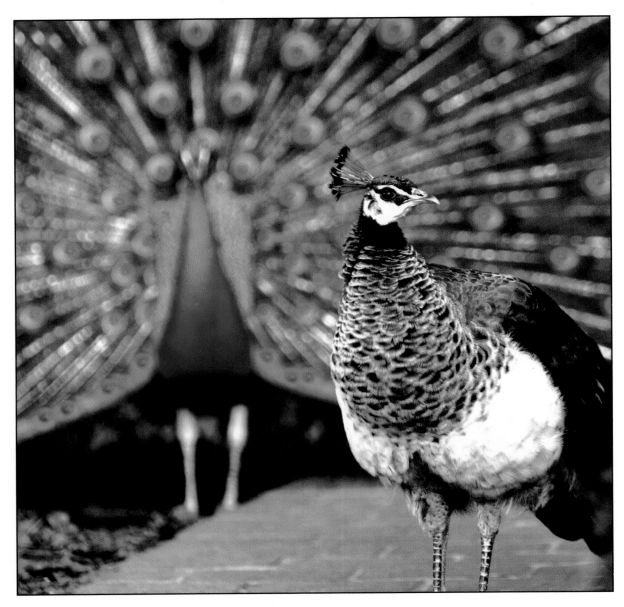

Males put their tails up and proudly "display,"
impressing the hens in March, April, and May.

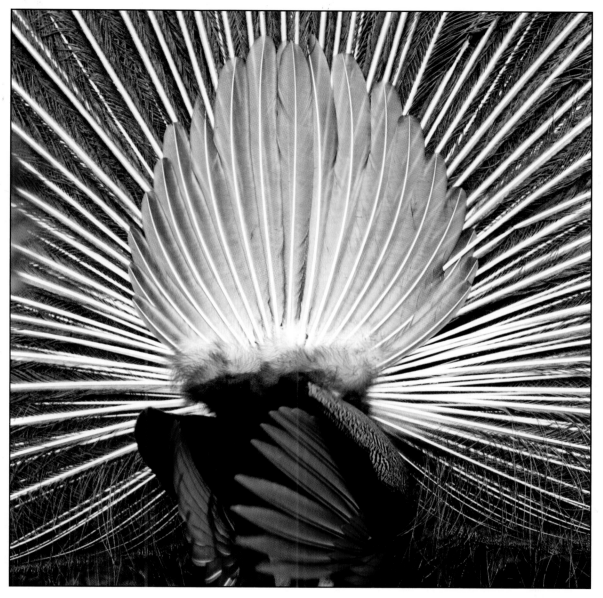

Dancing and stomping, those show-offs flounce by,
shaking their tails to catch a hen's eye.

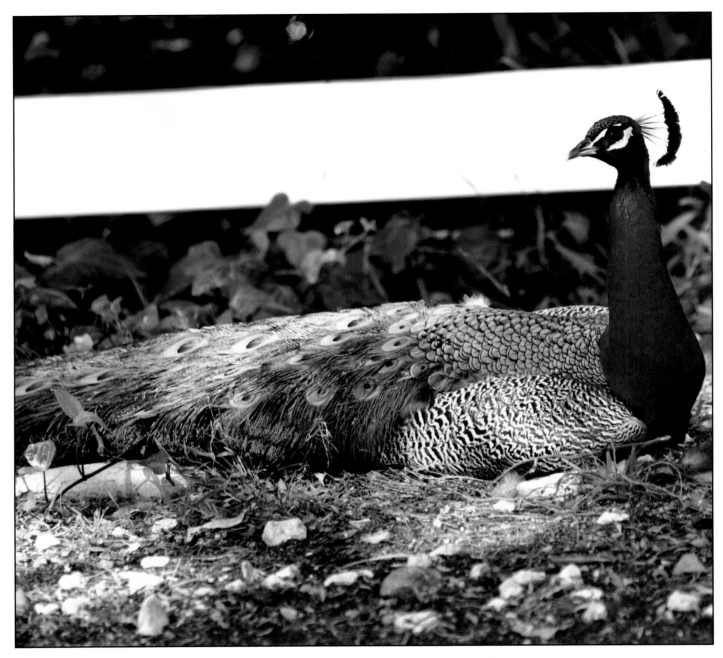

Then the peacocks relax. They slow down and rest. Now it's time for the peahens to start making nests.

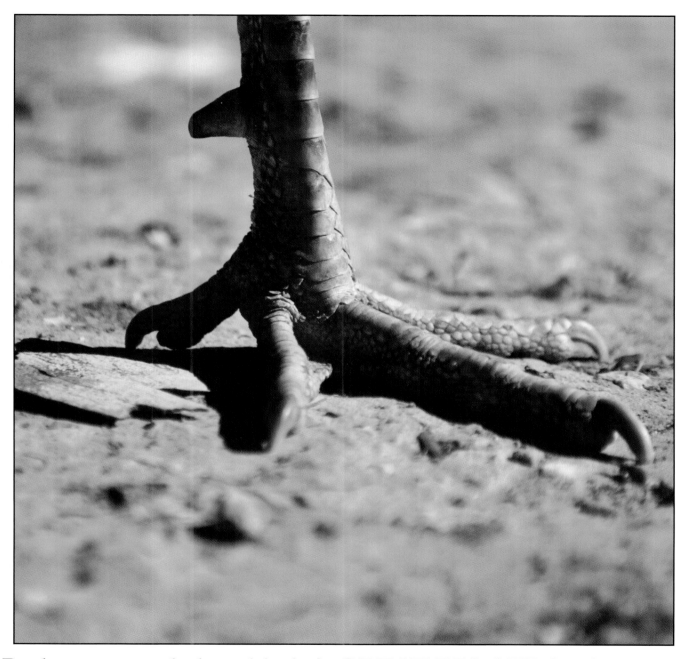

Peahens scrape holes with their **GREAT BIG STRONG FEET**. Some sticks, a few leaves, and the nursery's complete.

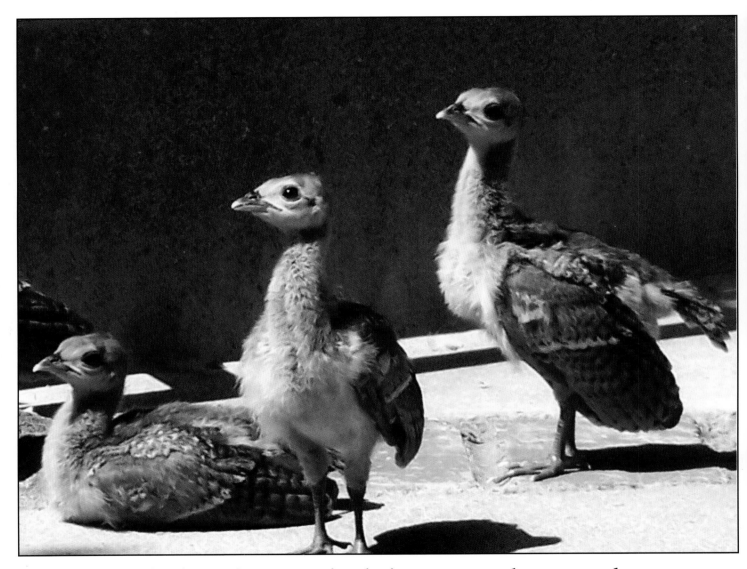

The hens lay eggs in their nests on the ground,
keeping them safe 'til the babies come round.

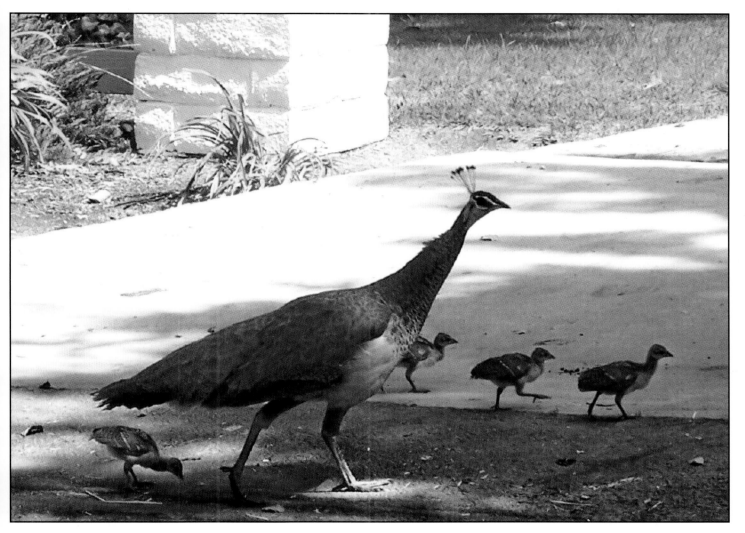

The little chicks eat and walk right away,
following mom, too frightened to stray.

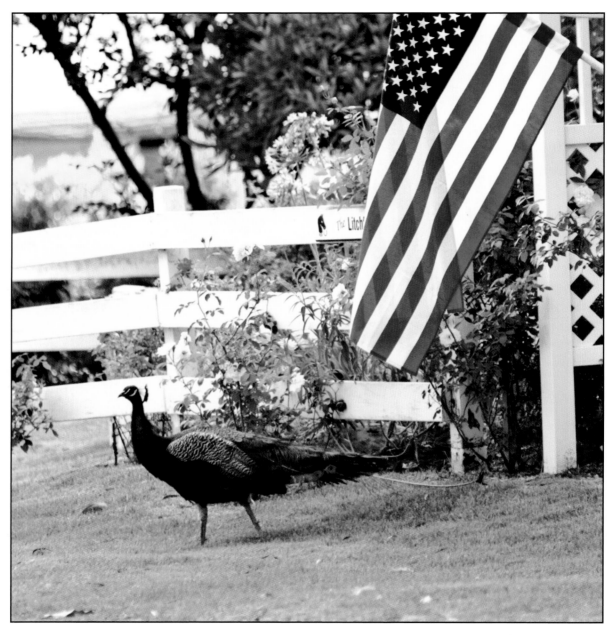

They love Palos Verdes where they can be found
in canyons and neighborhoods roaming around,

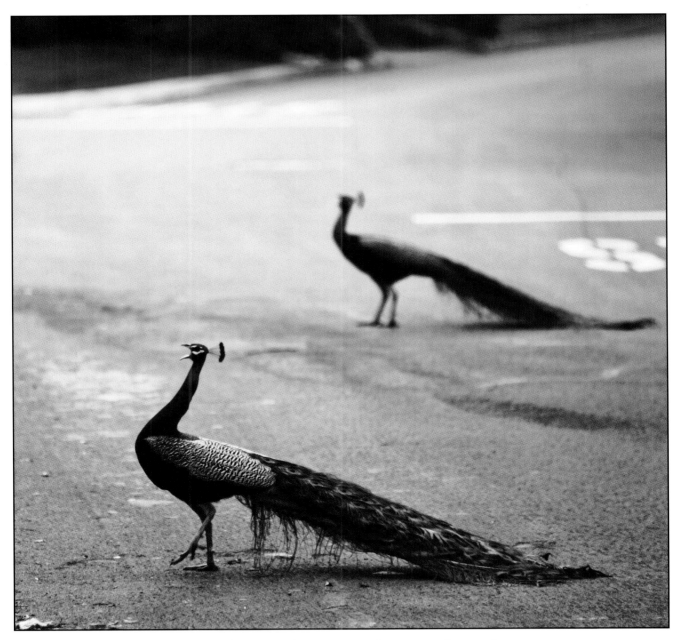

marching through gardens and strutting down streets,
crying "Arrrondt! Arrrondt!" to people they meet.

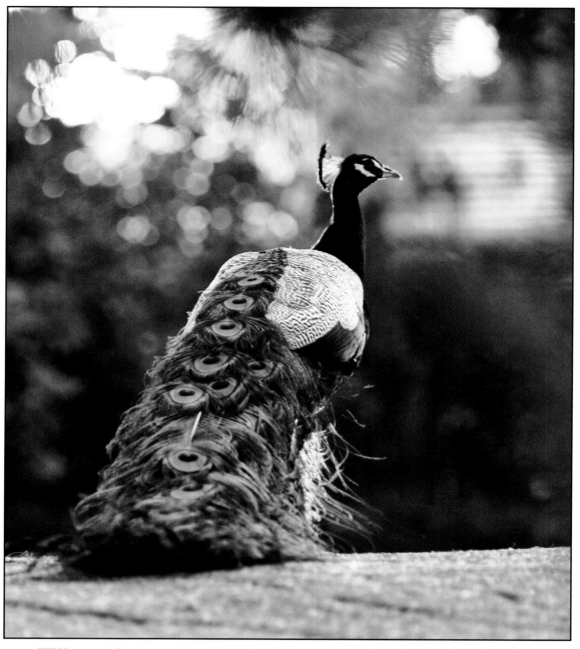

When the sun goes down and it's time for bed,
they return to their trees — those sleepyheads.

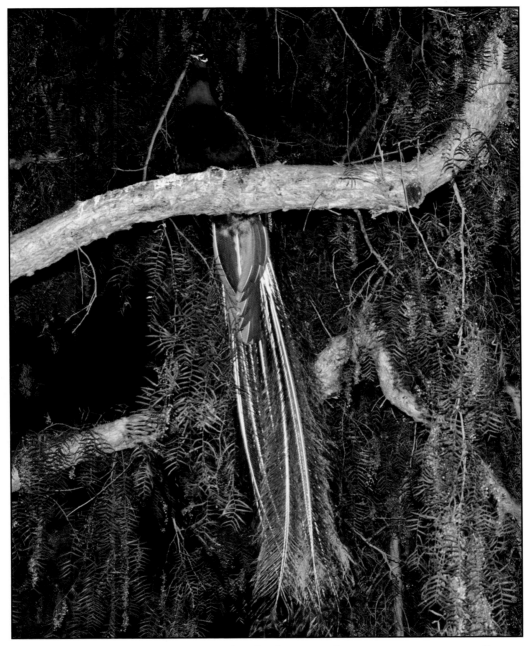

And when they are settled they give one more shout,
"Good night! Sleep tight! Hold on! Don't fall out!"

Afterword

In 1879, Lucky Baldwin imported three pairs of peacocks from India to his estate in Arcadia, California. One day Frank Vanderlip, Sr. visited his good friend Lucky at his estate and fell in love with the colorful birds. Years later, Lucky's daughter Anita sent Mr. Vanderlip peacocks for his own collection of exotic birds on his Rancho Palos Verdes estate.

A thoughtful gift of a few peacocks from one friend to another in the early 1900s developed into colonies of semi-domestic peacocks spread out today over the Palos Verdes Peninsula.

And I would like to thank Mrs. Elin Vanderlip, daughter-in-law of Frank Vanderlip, for her interest, help and support.

Acknowledgments

My special thanks and love to my husband, Victor, for his love, support and enthusiasm while I was writing and researching peacocks for over two years. My love, appreciation and recognition to my children and their spouses--Jackie, Steve, Mitzi, Tory, Maureen, Jennifer and Mark--for their insight, encouragement and help. I am full of gratitude and love for my grandchildren who accompanied me on peacock adventures and let me view the peacocks through their eyes. They were the inspiration for this book.

And my brother Bob Dellinger—thank you for your support and encouragement.

Thank you, Betty Lucas, for your interest in my book, your encouragement and your advice along the way.

Thank you to Captain Mark Velez—the very first person I interviewed.

I couldn't have written this book without the help of Jean Shriver and The Millie Ames Tuesday Writing Group at the Peninsula Library.

I am grateful to the Surfwriters Group and my beloved Redondo Beach Monday Writers' Group. Your insight, edits, companionship, and encouragement helped me so much. Thank you, Emma, Devi, Karen and Lia.

I am so appreciative for the interest, support and love from my CORE reading group. Grace, Dorothy, Becky, Kathleen, Barb, Tami and Jan-- thank you for your faith in me.

Special thanks to Maria Gonzales for her love, support, and belief, that my dream of a book about peacocks could come true.

Thank you, Deborah Mott, for your time, your interest, your wisdom, and your information and for protecting the peacocks on the peninsula for us all.

To the Palos Verdes Library Staff, I am grateful to Marjeanne Blinn, Local History Librarian, for making sure the historical facts in the book are accurate, to Laura Henry, Young Readers Department Manager, for her interest and enthusiasm, and to Julie Mattix, Finance Director, for her humor and support along the way.

Hugs and love to Carrie Concha of Brighter Days Montessori School, the staff and the children for letting me "try out" my book at the school. Thank you so much.

And thanks to Kiersten Hazard for her editing skills and to Trent Hazard Giacalone for perfecting his "peacock cry" and fearlessly teaching it to family, friends and strangers!